HEART ON PAPER

EMMA SERIO

*to the ones who broke my heart
and to the ones that healed me
to all the people who came in my life
and left an impact or a scar*

this book is for you

*to anyone fighting in the dark,
i see you <3*

innocence stolen from her when she was still so young.
had no choice but to grow up overnight,
to dry her own tears and pick herself up off the floor.
called a liar, a storyteller, and a burden,
yet she found it in her to speak her truth.

could never fully trust those around her who should protect her,
watching adults turn her life upside down
she was still silently hopeful.

hopeful that one day she would be able to
to find herself and shine as she was meant to.

i don't remember much about that girl
the girl i was before this one,
the memories of her life
lost in a traumatized mind and body,
but i do know she existed.
i know she is me.
i carry her around with me everywhere.

i know we are healing,
because we are here now.

      -e.s.

HEART ON PAPER

i hide my secrets well,
they are hidden
in the very back corners of my mind

i don't allow for people
who never bother to know me
know me or my secrets

you could dig for centuries
and never strike my core

    -   *e.s*

people are often left in shock
when they discover something new about my life,
words such as, *when did that happen?*
escape from their mouths
i often smile and do not respond
you never took the time to get to know me
why would it come as a surprise
when you learn you may not know the whole story.

- *e.s*

my depression was not
oversleeping and messy rooms,
it wasn't
unwashed hair and excessive crying
it wasn't constant sadness and despair.

my depression was fun,
had a mind of it's own,
it was a party animal and reckless nights,
it was a rebel and delusional,
it was feeling unstoppable and avoiding all
responsibilities,
it was a sleep avoidant and rage filled.
it was powerful and did not care to slow down.

look out for this type of depression,
it knows how to disguise itself as something so
normalized.

depression does not fit into a box,
it is different for every mind.
depression is so dangerous like that.

    -   *e.s*

HEART ON PAPER

we spent our whole lives running away,
we escaped obstacle after obstacle,
we kept running until we were so far
that the darkness couldn't follow us,

or so we thought,
but to our surprise,
the darkness caught up to us,
and it brought along many new friends
many new obstacles to jump through.

what now,
do we run again?
or do we stand together and finally combat our past.
i think we are learning,
that you could spend all your days running
but the moment you stop to catch your breath
it will all catch up to you.
stop running before your feet are pulled from under you.

-    e.s

time was not on our side,
it did not give us enough time
to evolve as we should of,
time ripped you from me so fast,
and now all we have is our memories,
we can not turn back time.

- *e.s*

HEART ON PAPER

i come home after a long day
exhausted, drained
i look for you to recharge me

the lights turned off and everyone's asleep
still you're not here to hold me.

what happened to the nights
we stayed up talking until the sun came up
what happened to you holding me so tight
the weight of the day melted off my shoulders
what happened to always having a shoulder to cry on

you can pretend you don't care,
pretend it's different
but i know you think of us,
and wish you could turn back time.

what a shame

    - *letters to him*

HEART ON PAPER

my life is lived in survival mode.
my mind is working on autopilot.

i am functioning and moving through every motion,
but i am not connected. not like i should be.

life is happening around me right now,
i am watching my life from above, i am not the character.

-*e.s.*

i don't want to ask surface level questions
i don't want to feel the need to fill the empty space
between our words with remarks that have no significance

i don't want to be called beautiful
only when i am lying beneath you naked
and then never told again

i want our souls to connect
i want to look into you and feel safe

i want to lay with you in silence
and feel your heartbeat
i want a future
i want to feel so much love that my heart explodes.

i've felt this kind of love,
or so i believed,
and now that it's gone,
i don't want to go looking and scanning faces
in a game of trial and error until i find that love again.

   - *finding love in our generation is exhausting*

closing a chapter of my life i thought i would never have to close.
i had no say,
my body followed where i was told to go
even though my heart longed to stay.
my home with all that i've ever known
ripped away from me overnight,

i will never forget the pain as i boarded the plane.
as i boarded the plane that would take me to a new world,
a new life. a life we had to start from scratch to build.

i've grown up.

i've accepted what has happened.

but the little girl that lives within me
will never outgrow that pain
she will always want to go home and stay.

    - *homesick.*

i *now* cope with therapy,

i try to tell you that there is more on the other side,
i ask you to join me on that side

i try to tell you that you can get high on life without a hallucigen,
i try to show you all the color that will return to your life,
i tell you that there is *real happiness* once you throw out the happiness in a bottle.

i try.

as i try to heal you,
you try to bring me back down, down to your coping ways,
you swear by them but i swore to never fall so low again,
you say that i'll fall again one day
and while that may be true,
i still believe in trying.

you say i've changed
and you are right,
i want more in life, then what we had.

as i put one foot in front the other,
you continue to put one foot in the grave.

    - *recovery is possible, i promise*

i've always wanted to be strong,
i've always done everything to protect my heart.

so i built walls,
i built miles and miles of thick walls,
walls that covered every single crack, for every single aspect of life.

but i think i am learning,
that strength does not come from your ability to build walls,
it comes from your ability to break them down,
to allow the light to shine through the cracks.

-healing

i memorized every tattoo and every scar on your skin,
i studied it as if it were my own body,

i memorized every wound in your heart,
so i could learn how to patch each wound up with my love.

but now all i have is scars
the scars you left me with
with no more patches left for myself.

    - *heartbreak*

HEART ON PAPER

some people are a breath of fresh air
others take all the air out of your lungs until you can no longer breathe,
you get to choose who you are around,

do you want to breathe?

- *e.s.*

you are older and wiser,
that's your trick.
you convince her because you are older and wiser,
she thought she would be safe, that you would always protect her.
you wait until the day you can claim her as your own
you say all the right things with your mouth
but your eyes are filled with the truth,
filled with anger. filled with *power.*
the power you use to manipulate her into following you into a cage,
a cage where you convince her she's safe, she'd never be alone.
until you walk out of the cage and lock her in without escape.
she went from believing you were her protector
to knowing that *you* are actually what she needs protecting from.
but she is stuck, with no way out.
    -   *betrayal*

HEART ON PAPER

when they ask about you
i'll tell them
that you were the brightest star in the whole sky
that lit up the darkness,
and without you the world is forever dark

   -    *e.s.*

nothing i did was ever enough for you
i have accepted that.

but that does not mean i do not break
everytime i am reminded that i am not worthy of your love

- *e.s*

i learned i could not beg someone to stay
when they chose to leave,
even if that person's sole job was to stay.

-e.s

as much as i want to be able
to be cut loose from you
i can't seem to cut off the chains,
i can't seem to let you go,

for my love for you
is far too deep and far too strong
to ever allow myself to cut you off.

-   *e.s.*

i get enough sleep
if we are counting the thirty minute naps
we take to prevent us from passing out
in between daily tasks.

i shower once a day
with the lights off, as i can not seem to
allow myself to be *alone* with myself.

i socialize a good amount
but how much of it are we sober for?

no i'm fine, i promise
please, when are we going to be
honest?

- *conversations with inner self*

i'm okay. i promise,
i have everything under control.

okay, now repeat it 100 times.

- *fake it till you make it*

i don't like this part of healing.

the part that makes your old habits look comforting,

the part that makes you question
every step you've taken.

the part where your mind tells you
to forget about recovery, to fall on your knees
and surrender.

but you have to remember the reason
why you chose to recover,

you have to remember,
healing isn't always linear.

-    e.s.

when my physical presence is
no longer here,
maybe that day,
you'll actually believe someone,
when they tell you the *pain* they are in.

-    *e.s*

HEART ON PAPER

everyone warned me,
but i did not care.

i chased you.
i wanted you.
i wanted you so desperately
i ignored every sign telling me to run the other way.
i gave and gave and gave, waiting for the day you would choose me.

it took over two years to figure out,
love just doesn't work that way.

-     e.s.

HEART ON PAPER

it feels illegal to love someone other than you.
for so long, i have had blinders on only for you
i walk where you walk
i follow you anywhere you go.

i keep dwelling on the past.
every day and night,
you consume my mind.

dreaming.
fantasizing.
wishing.
dwelling,
over and over,
it's draining.

it would have been much simpler
if I hadn't fallen for you in the first place.

    -e.s.

i was just starting to recover,
i was starting to believe that i could go without you,
but then you looked at me.
why did you have to look at me like that.
    -    e.s

HEART ON PAPER

there is nothing beautiful about
restless nights and bruises under my eyes,
there is nothing beautiful about
losing consciousness and feeling your heart skip a beat,
do not romanticize
that i can no longer stare into the mirror without breaking down,
my headspace is not beautiful.
my headspace does not make me strong.
i am mentally exhausted and drained,
there is nothing beautiful about that.
- *e.s*

HEART ON PAPER

some names will always be cursed,
i will always look up when i hear their name.
maybe one day i can hear their names without crumbling.
   -   e.s

"we were too young for this"
correction.
i was too young for this.
you on other hand,
were a grown adult.
you knew exactly what you were doing.
don't get that twisted.
    -   e.s

HEART ON PAPER

maybe next time you are mad,
i'll put a picture of my face up on the wall for you to run your fist into.
because i am your favorite thing you like to hurt.
and once your done hurting me,
i'll get a new picture and put that up on the wall to cover the hole
so that all your madness stays hidden.
-    e.s

do you stay because you love them?
or do you stay because
you're scared *they* don't love you.

- e.s.

woke up
and repeated the cycle of pain.

because pain felt comfortable,
and at this point in her life,

she was scared not to feel it.

— *e.s.*

you watched as i lit myself on fire,
you watched as if i was only there for your entertainment,
as if my life meant nothing,

you watched me light my match,
set myself on fire, and simply walked away.

you watched me turn into ashes,

now i am left with the remains of myself

    -   e.s.

their broken hearts left a bad taste on my tongue
they have new loves, new lives, new memories.
two separate homes, with two separate families.
i am the only reminder
of their relationship

my broken sense of love
for I have never seen it.

    -   *a child of divorce*

all the sudden
one day,
you wake up older,
not wiser, just older.

you're alone with a younger version of yourself

staring at a childhood
you no longer remember

    -   *growing up*

dissociating is a strange feeling.
physically trapped in your body,
your mind being elsewhere,
dragging you into the memories of your past.

- *e.s.*

HEART ON PAPER

today i finally stood still,
i looked out into the horizon
i felt the wind in my hair,
i breathed in the fresh air
when i came to a realization,
we live so much of our lives in our minds,
we forget all about our bodies.
we forget to be where our feet are.

    -   *e.s*

i need to sleep
i know i do.

but how do i sleep
when my mind is shuffling
mountains of memories throughout my brain.
reminding me of my fears and paranoias.

tears trickle down my face,

as i lay there silently,
forcing my eyes to shut.
and dreading the nightmares
that i know i will have.

    - *insomnia*

how can you leave,
throw me to the side with no explanation,
destroy everything we were busy building,
go off and begin to build something new with someone new,
and expect me to be the one to beg to have you in my life?
- *e.s*

the feeling of being alone.
people don't understand
it's the only time where i can be myself
no pretending,
no forced conversations
no awkward silence

just me.
my own comfort

    -   *e.s*

is it the physical feeling i crave?
or the thought that
if someone knew they might care.

- *self harm*

what i needed from you had no cost.
i didn't ask to be placed in this world
and you did everything possible to show me

that i in fact did not belong.
unfortunately i never got to be his little girl,
the little girl who made his smile light up,

i was unwanted and thrown to the side
my very existence was disregarded.
you were not around to help guide me
not around to tell me you were proud of me.

you hurt me before i even knew what hurt felt like,
I want the life back you all so selfishly stole.
i cried and cried by the door waiting for the day you decided to come back,
but you didn't come back, and so i wiped off my own tears.

growing up, i've looked for you in many different faces,
warped love found in all the wrong places.
scared to love, cause I don't know how,
I'm all grown up so what do I do now?

one thing I do know to be clear:
all i want is to be able to love without fear.

    - *distant father's daughter*

instilled in our minds that men are always the heroes in
the story
my mother proved that wrong.

she protected me from the big world
she saved me from myself
she is the light at the end of the tunnel
she restores my faith in love
she restores my faith in motherhood,

there is no love quite like that of my mother,
she loved me before i understood what love was,
she that never has given up on me,

   -   *my mother, my hero*

no one seems to understand how i can possibly
love you as much as i do,

you've made mistakes,
no doubts there,

and as much as i wish things were different for us,
for the way life went for us,
i cannot go back into the past and change anything,
and neither can you.

so i choose to live in the present with you,
hopeful that you have learned from your mistakes
hopeful that there is still *hope* for our relationship
because all i really know,
is that you are my bloodline,
where i receive my name from,
and that is something no amount of mistakes, or distance
can ever take away from us.

    -   *i am still my father's daughter*

at the end of everything,
we stayed standing.
even when home around us was under destruction,
when hammers were swinging and fires were burning.
even when home was ripped from us, and we lost the roof over our heads.
when we had no roots to keep us grounded,
we remained.
we could lose everything as long as we held on to each other,
we let everything fly away into the storm, as long as we held on to each other.
and when we looked around at the complete chaos of our lives,
we smiled because even though we had just lost everything,
we still had home. we still had us.
look at us now.

    - *letter to my sister*

HEART ON PAPER

i sit on my floor,
wearing the hoodie you gave me,

breathing you in,
a reminder that we once existed,
that we once were something bigger than i ever believed
to be possible.

i sit here and cry until i have drained my eyes of every
drop
i sit here and weep until i no longer miss you,
i sit here and pretend that my heart doesn't still miss you.

    -    *e.s*

HEART ON PAPER

i don't know what to do,
you left your mark across my heart,
you held me and promised to never let me go,

come back to me,
i can't lose again.

let me hold you,
and never let you go

-e.s

HEART ON PAPER

i hope that one day,
my mind and i will be at peace,

i am patiently waiting for the day
my mind decides to be on my side

i hope one day, even if it takes
the rest of my life,

i hope one day
my mind starts listening to
what my heart needs.

- *e.s*

HEART ON PAPER

when you look into my eyes,
do you really see me?

do you see beyond my eyes,
take the time to get to know the person standing in front of you?

or do you just see what you want to see.
do you take what you want,
leaving my eyes full of tears?

-e.s

HEART ON PAPER

im only a phone call away you say,
yet you never seem to pick up your phone.

you mean everything to me you say,
yet you never seem to ask about me.

i never want to hurt you,
yet *you* are the one that taught me what hurt feels like

    -   *e.s*

HEART ON PAPER

it's funny,
they say the older you get, the wiser you are
yet i keep making the same mistakes.

the older i get the more i repeat.
the more i regret.

how old must i be before i learn,
you cannot beg people to change.
you cannot fix what wants to stay broken

you cannot put your trust into people so easily.
i can't seem to figure it out
no matter how old i am,
making mistakes seems to be my default.
- *e.s*

HEART ON PAPER

i defended you, for everything,
i let you take everything from me,
all i hoped for,
is for you to at least stand with me.

instead, you stood behind me
you let me take all the punches
you let me take all your burdens
you let me take all your problems
you let me take all the blame

i let you bleed all over me,

i let you knock me down, repeatedly,
yet you never lended me a hand to pick me back up.

- *e.s*

they say,

HEART ON PAPER

talk to others
we care
we want to help
i love you

unfortunately these sentences
mean nothing to me,

i can't seem to open my mouth and talk,
i can't seem to tell you everything i want to tell you,
even if maybe, if i opened up, if i broke down my walls
after so many years, i would feel so much better,

but everyone has so much going on,
how can someone possibly have the time to listen to what
i have to say
i need them to listen to me

where do i start?
how do i reassure them that i am okay
even if i'm not.
see,
as much as i want to talk
i can't seem to bring myself to open my mouth,
because as much as i want you to know the truth
i dont have the reassurance that you won't judge me,
that i am not a burden to you.

so i stay quiet.

- *e.s*

you matter,
i am so sorry

i love you.
please do not leave

i wish i could change the way
you see yourself

don't ever go quiet again.

- *words i needed to hear*

HEART ON PAPER

your body is art
unique, one of a kind.
carefully painted on a canvas

no two paintings are the same,
each comes with a unique set of characteristics.

divinely designed
one of a kind

    -   *e.s*

you are a star
but not in the meaning that you're the best or the winner.

you are a star
providing light through all the darkness

giving direction to those who are lost,
giving hope to all those who look up looking for a reason

a sense of tranquility and purpose,
you are a star

    -    *e.s*

you gain your power
in the moments
when you're falling to your knees
draining your eyes
of every tear they may hold
when you feel your soul change.

in that moment
with that pain
when you look at yourself in the mirror
you realize how strong you truly are.

- *letters from me, to you*

i dig my nails into my skin
i feel my chest tense up
memories of the past flood into my mind,
thoughts rush into my head,
i feel it throughout my whole body.
i focus on making myself invisible in a crowd of people,
i distract myself with pain
any kind of pain i can

    -   *anxiety*

it only takes one bad memory
to dull all the good memories we had

- *e.s*

HEART ON PAPER

there aren't enough bottles of alcohol in the world
that could drown out the sound of your voice
that lives within my head,

there aren't nearly enough drugs in the universe
that could make me forget the feeling
of how it felt to lay with you and feel safe.

- *e.s*

HEART ON PAPER

its my fault,
for trying to fix you.
for trying to fix every broken person

sometimes i was successful,
but not with you.
i tried so hard,
but your never wanted to be fixed
it was my fault for believe that with you
i could be successful and save you from yourself.

-    *e.s*

i know i shouldn't but i can't help myself.
i feel comfort by sitting on the cold floor,
alone with myself, with my thoughts,
going further and further into the dark
i feel comfort in feeling stomach eat away at itself,
comfort in floating up to the clouds, as high up as possible
and dreaming of never coming back down

- *unhealthy habits*

HEART ON PAPER

i construct walls around my heart
not to keep my heart safe
but to see who cares enough to break down those barriers

i keep all my secrets covered
to see who will finally prove me wrong,
allowing me to let them in.

i am sad to report that i still haven't found that kind of
care i need
i give
and all i get is hurt
in return

-   *e.s*

HEART ON PAPER

if i show you my feelings,
how deep my heart has been hurt,
i'm too sensitive.
i'm being dramatic.

if i'm cold and uptight,
i'm not in touch with myself,
im insensitive.

where is the balance,
why do i have to fit in this box
to feel normal.

    -e.s

i've been holding my breath around you,
walking as quietly as possible
completing every task before you even ask me,

making sure everything is in order for you,
because i think i would rather make myself small in order to keep you,
rather than standing up tall and losing you.

    -   *e.s*

HEART ON PAPER

i'm tired of swimming all the way up to the surface
getting that breath of air in my lungs,
seeing all the colors that life has to offer,
just to be pushed underwater again,
to be pushed and pulled all the way down to the dark
bottom.

- *depression*

i have spent hours perfecting my smile,
making sure my eyes get bigger,
that my laugh sounds real,
allowing for others to see what i want them to see.

i have to say,
it is exhausting perfecting a version of yourself,
that is not entirely true.

- *e.s*

best friends until we die,
spent every day together,
knew all of each others deepest moments,

best friends until we die,
 i guess we never did break that promise.

we were the best of friends until you took your last breath
even though i had lost you to addiction many months
before you took your final breath,
never for one second did i stop loving you.

best friends until we die.

   -    *e.s*

i left my hometown,
i thought when that happened it would've meant
that i could begin to heal from you,

me and you combined are a *disaster,*
you've got me under your spell,
i do anything you tell me to do,
and when i listen to you, that is when you tell me
you love me.

if you fall, you bring me down with you,

the problem here is that i do not care,
i go down with you so easily,
because as much as i don't want to
i love you.

you have this hold on me,
and when i'm back in that same town
i always come crawling back to you,
and I always end up falling.

    - *when will i let him go*

something i have learned is
you will never get over it,

you learn to live with it

- *e.s*

i don't know if i'll ever be enough for my own brain.

if i'll never be enough for myself,
how am i supposed to believe i am
enough for anyone else?

    - *e.s*

HEART ON PAPER

it is hard to focus
when your brain and heart are constantly at war.

it is hard to breathe,
when your brain convinces you that your every move is wrong.

it is hard to trust,
when your heart has been broken in half,
and poorly sewn back together.

- *e.s*

HEART ON PAPER

my heart takes things to far,
i see the signs when i should stop caring.
my brain sees the danger yet my heart runs directly towards it.
my brain and my heart are constantly at war,
like having an angel and devil sitting on my shoulder
one tells me to stop and one tells me to go.

HEART ON PAPER

you laugh at me when i cry,
you push me over and hold me down,

you pick me up,
just to push me back down.

still i look up at you
give you that broken smile i always give you,
even though i am so close to giving up on you i hold on,

i hold on to that person you are behind the rage,
that person you were
before you began to pump your veins with poison.

i hold on, hopeful that i can find that version of you
that lives within your heart
and make it permanent.

   -    e.s

i stare with pity,
my body once strong and confident
is no longer mine.

changed to fit into a standard,
morphed by comments of others.

- *e.s*

HEART ON PAPER

why do i love you when
all you do is hurt me?

- *e.s*

you tell me you will do anything to help
yet i am the one at the end of the night
picking myself up off the floor.
- *e.s*

every generation before, dealt the cards for you,
trauma passed on from person to person until it reached you,
swallowed you whole
no wonder it feels so heavy,
you are not only carrying your own hardships,
but also the ones of every person before you.
give yourself grace.

- *e.s*

you didn't fully love me, not like i've been told someone should love.
but i didn't love myself, not the way i've been told i should love myself.
so i guess we finally agreed on one thing.

- *e.s*

fighting to keep yourself together every single day is exhausting,
but so is choosing to recover.
because for some reason, recovery in my life is always only temporary,
it always comes back and each time it gets stronger and stronger.
-    e.s

it is never too late to come back to me.
i will never run out of second chances.
no matter what you do,
i will still find it in me to find the good in you
and drag it out into the world as best as i can.
i don't give up on people easily,
ever.

although that can't be said about others.
i've been given up on more times than i can count,
told there is no more love, no more support they can give me
that it is up to me to make a change.
they leave, they give up
they tell me i am a lost cause.
these are the same people that come crawling back every time they need something.
and with open arms i gracefully and willinging take them in with no hesitation.

- *e.s*

HEART ON PAPER

days pass by like a blur,
im left alone with my thoughts
they control me,
they are the ones that make all the decisions.

i feel drained lately
not tired, just mentally drained.
i interact with others to be polite.

- *e.s*

i love when i am at peace with myself
but sometimes it gets lonely,
i feel like i'm stuck on a shelf,
time passes by to quickly and to slowly

    -    *e.s*

HEART ON PAPER

i knew something had to change,
i knew because loving you felt like a blade to my skin
whereas letting you go felt like flying,

how twisted must i be
to choose to continuously bleed,
instead of flying away.

- *e.s*

HEART ON PAPER

it's me or him.
i cannot save us both.
i've tried,
i've tried to swim down to the bottom, and bring him back
up to the surface,
but he always ends up holding me down,
our souls combined,
are too heavy for only me to carry.
and i have run out of ideas
on how to convince him to swim.
but foolish me,
i allow him to hold me underwater.
i shall wait with him
until he is ready to swim again.
    -    *e.s*

it was not easy to be happy,
happy that they got everything they took from us,
happy that it was so easy for them to move on.
i silently hope everyday that they know
the pain they caused,
the people they knocked over to stand up tall.
i bite my tongue,
i smile and listen to their stories
listen to everything they have accomplished since pushing me down,
it's not easy,
but still my response when i open my mouth is
i'm so happy for you.

- e.s

the cards are not in my favor,
the stars have not aligned,
fate has been so cruel,

but i have to hold on that one day
things will change,
one day i will pull the right card,
i will see the stars shine
i will prove that fate does not determine your outcome.
i'll hold on to that.
    - *one day it'll all be okay*

HEART ON PAPER

i'll be the villain in your story,
i'll push you to get better,
i'll be the friend you can shout at,
ill be your punching bag,
the friend you can hate,
i'll be the person to get mad for you,
to advocate for you,
to find the resources for you,
i'll be there to bring you back to reality when you have drifted too far,
i'll push you out of your comfort zone to help you.
because i know you need it,
i know your heart is secretly thanking me.
go on, tell everyone you hate me,
tell everyone i am too involved,
i'll stand there and smile as i see you slowly become you again.
if that makes me the villain in your story,
ill gladly take that role.
- *e.s*

one day, you are going to think back to this time of your life
and you are going to realize that you have once again conquered an impossible obstacle,
and i promise it will make you smile.

- *e.s*

take that day off,
remind yourself that you are the most important thing in your life.
allow yourself an hour,
and hour to allow your brain to breathe.
allow yourself to not have responsibilities for a moment
to be with yourself in peace.
heal your pain.
you are the only one that knows how much you bleed.

- *letter to the reader*

watching a storm is calming
because you know the storm will pass
and soon the sun will shine
you know that flowers will bloom
and that life will return to normal

but, will the storm
inside my head
ever pass?

    -   *e.s*

HEART ON PAPER

please be gentle with me,
please handle me with care,
please do not raise your voice at me,
please do not be cruel to me,
please do not lie,
please do not hurt me,
please do not say goodbye,
please.

- *e.s*

you deserve to be here,
you deserve to feel everything this world as to offer to you
yes, there will be darkness
there will be days that feel as the world has turned it's back on you
that you are falling from the sky,
but you can only have the highs with the lows,
you can only go up once you have hit the floor.
we live in a beautiful world.
it would be a tragedy
if you were to leave it.
stay.

- *letter to the reader*

i believe that
no drink is free.
there is always a price to pay.
they always expect something more
something to come after that drink

   -   *don't trust it, don't trust anyone*

HEART ON PAPER

sleeping with the door locked,
constantly looking over my shoulders,
flinching at loud sounds,
mastering the art of makeup,
sweaty palms from too much eye contact,
broken bottles and picture frames,
degrading nicknames,
loud silence.

these are all the things you left me with,
reminders of you.
- *e.s*

HEART ON PAPER

it took,
ten months of not being able to sleep through the whole night.
nine months of living with flashbacks of you.
eight weeks of having to see you while panicking internally.
seven days for you to completely fade from my skin.
six months of therapy to try and erase you.
five people to convince you to walk away.
four days of me hiding out in my room.
three hours of nonstop crying afterwards.
two months of dissociation.

all because for one minute
you decided to take your anger,
out on my body.
    -   e.s

my younger self,
i've taught her two lessons.
life is so tough,
but you are so much tougher.
i know she is smiling up at me.

    -   *e.s*

if the mirror had feelings,
i wonder if it would be hurt by the
words you say to it

- *e.s*

HEART ON PAPER

my younger self
was asked to hold onto hardships that were not her own.
asked to be a shoulder to cry on,
for shoulders much older than hers.
now i have to act surprised when others tell me,
i am older than my years.
    -   *e.s*

the more time you spend in the dark,
the more your eyes start to adjust to the darkness,
the darkness starts to feel comfortable,

now imagine the light gets turned on,
it is supposed to hurt.

this is recovery.

   -   *e.s*

i cover my body with baggy clothes now,

i can no longer look at myself in the mirror for longer than
a few seconds.

i can't eat alone,
i'm never alone,
the constant voice that tells me
that i will never be enough
makes me put my fork down.

i'm in a constant battle
i'm constantly trying to walk forward
but this illness has a chain wrapped around my ankle
and I drag *her* with me everywhere i go.

i've tried to break of the chain
with every possible method
out there, but
she is unbreakable

so i cover my body with baggy clothes now.

    - *disordered eating*

from one drowning victim to another,
i promise,
you have the choice
to stop holding onto the water

    - *e.s*

i don't think we were in love anymore,
we were just in love
with not being alone.

- *e.s*

how would i explain that i'm not going anywhere;
but i'm not okay,

how do i explain that i want to wake up in the morning,
but silently hope that i can sleep through the whole day,

surviving your own head.
the kind of bravery no one ever mentions,
no awards are given out,
no round of applause.

    - *surviving your head*

oh don't worry it's just a cry for help
so why didn't you help her?

- *e.s*

many nights crying wondering why i wasn't enough for you,
but only you know that.
i can't change the past. neither can you, and i do not hold that against you.
you have never been one to look back into the past, and i can respect that.
i didn't hesitate to give him a second chance to build back up what was broken. why?
why did i not hesitate to build that bond with you, why didn't i make you work for it a little harder.
i think that deep down i would rather have a strained relationship with you
 than to have none at all.

    -   *letter to my father*

i know i am a very sensitive person.
it's actually one of the traits i have grown to love about myself.
i allow myself to feel pain, happiness, anger, any emotion because growing up i always pushed those feelings aside. with that sensitivity in me i have learned to do my best to make sure my words don't upset anyone, i tell white lies to try and avoid making others feel hurt.
but over time i learned that even an ugly truth is better than a good white lie

- *e.s*

HEART ON PAPER

my old self
had to die

how beautiful it is
when i let go
of old things
that had to die

- *old habits*

you have no idea
what had to burn and break
to become this version of me

   -   *e.s*

i screamed so loud,
but i understand now,
no one can hear you when you are underwater.
- *e.s*

i am not proud of all the decisions my past self made,
but this version of myself would never exist if it wasn't for her,
so instead of holding onto the guilt and resentment for her,
i choose to forgive her,
i thank her for who i am now.
- e.s

HEART ON PAPER

i can't sit still for more than a few moments
i can feel my heart begin to pound like
it's about to explode out of my chest

it feels as my stomach turns inside out
so i stand up
i do a few laps around the room
just to sit and return to
that awful feeling in my chest

my throat closes up
it feels like i can't breathe
like my head is slowly going underwater
i fall to my knees

all my memories all my weaknesses
start eating away at me

next i feel drops falling onto my leg
i look in the mirror
to find that i have been crying
without even noticing
and the room feels like
it is closing in on me

i hope it magically stops
but it doesn't
it continues

    - *panic attacks*

there is no where else i feel safest
than in your arms

the universe has tried
over and over
to pull us apart
but it never works

that is because you are the
comfort i look for

when you hold me
so tight in your arms
that the world disappears
you stroke my hair
and kiss me on the forehead
and remind me i'm safe

you give me your hoodies that i wear almost every single day
so that even when your gone
i have you attached to my body

so even if what we are is
far from perfect
i know one thing for sure,

there is no where else i feel safest
than in your arms

    - *my comfort person*

HEART ON PAPER

i hate that you dulled my smile,
i hate that you convinced me i am unlovable.
i am way too good to you,
i hate that you laugh at me,
convinced me i am weak when i am the opposite.
   -   *things i can't say out loud.*

HEART ON PAPER

there will be chapters of your life you hope you will
never have to relive.
there will be chapters in your life you hope will
never be spoken about again.
chapters that end before they have begun,
and chapters that drag on for what seems forever,

and in the moments you wish to rip out the pages,
start again on a fresh page,
erase the past,
know that erasing your story
will make it harder to see how far you have come,
one day you will read back on those chapters that made
life feel so heavy,
and smile to see how far you've come.
keep going,
keep going until you hit a chapter you will want to read
forever.
    -   *e.s*

how did your hands
remain so clean
after you shattered my heart in your hands?
did you not cut your skin
on any of my broken pieces?

    -    *e.s*

people always ask how your day is going,

and no matter how bad your day was
the answer will always be good

because it's easier to fake a smile than
to let down the walls you've been building up for a while.

- *e.s*

sometimes you think all you want is
to fade away,
to disappear.
but i think all you really need is
to be found,
to be seen.

- *e.s*

HEART ON PAPER

as much as you broke me down,
you gave me my toughest layers of skin,
you are the reason why i still believe it when i say i am resilient.
because of you i never have to doubt myself
when someone tells me i am strong.
surviving *you* has to be the biggest blessings in disguise.
    -   *e.s*

you played with my innocence,
like it was a game where you already knew
that you were the guaranteed winner.

- *e.s*

there are so many things that i would change,
so many things i said that i wish stayed unsaid,
i wish they stayed unsaid so that you did not have the
luxury of knowing everything about me,
giving you the upper hand to hurt me right where you
know it will sting.
- *e.s*

HEART ON PAPER

i wish i could go back
to a time
before i knew that evil existed.
a time where i didn't know
that evil could live within so many people.
before people took their evil out on me.
    -    *e.s*

it is okay
to be afraid
of what comes next.

you are allowed to
not have a plan.

life does not have
specific rules
as to how it shall be lived
live it in the way
that makes *your* heart happy

-    *e.s*

i always find myself saying i'm okay when it is clear that i am not.
i always find myself doing the opposite of what i know is good for me.
self-care requires so much time getting to know yourself, so i choose self destruction.

- *e.s*

HEART ON PAPER

my whole life i have been told,
stay strong for others, they need your strength.
i am learning,
you can only take so much of others pain
until the pain swallows you whole.
give yourself the same comfort you give others so freely
and do not apologize for it.

- *e.s*

HEART ON PAPER

i always find myself looking up to the sky,
i stop and think back to when the sky was just the sky.
the sky has so much more meaning now,
so much more meaning when you know small pieces of
your heart live there now.
-    e.s

HEART ON PAPER

i breathe in fresh air,
but you continued to breathe in the smoke from your cigarette,

i decided to come down from the clouds,
you decided to float up until there was no chance of you to come back down to earth,

i wish i could've taken you with me,
i wish i could've changed your mind

I wish you were still here, on earth with me.

- *missing you*

HEART ON PAPER

it's 3 am
there's nothing
not a single text
no "i got home safe"
after driving home under the influence
even tho i begged you to just spend the night
and sober up

i keep myself up all night
worrying
hoping the next text is from you
saying you *did* make it home safe
and not from someone else
telling me you *didn't* make it

-    *e.s*

i love you
i would do anything for you
and that is why
when things get tough
you push me aside
you push
and push
and push
me away
because i'll let you
i love you

    -   *e.s*

HEART ON PAPER

i fall for your tricks so easily every night,
every night that you greet me with a big smile,
followed with a big hug and a laugh that lights up the whole room,
you convince me you are better, you are happy,
something i have hoped you'd be for as long as i have known you.
i fall asleep at peace, relieved.
i hope that this is it, this is the time you have finally chosen recovery.

but then we wake up,
as if i have woken up from a dream that only exists in my fantasies,
you're you again.
sad, angry.
that spark in your eye is gone.

i'm met with my disappointment again,
it wasn't really you i was with the night before,
it was your addiction.
and your addiction does such a good job at convincing me you're okay.
- *e.s*

sometimes it feels as i will always come second,
i haven't found the feeling of being good enough,
i work on myself everyday
making sure i do not bleed on those who did not cut me,
i have tried to be transparent, to be my authentic self,
but yet i still come up second.

- *e.s*

they say they will be there for me
but they leave as soon
as i need them

they are nice to me
only if they want something

they say they love me
but never want to show it

    -    *e.s*

i grow,
i get better,
i smile more,
i finally see what normal is supposed to feel like,
and then i fall,
i cry,
i go quiet again.
this endless pattern is exhausting
    -   *e.s*

focus on filling each other with love instead of hate,
the world already is filled with hatred,
humanity needs to do better.
- *e.s*

holding a conversation these days feels draining,
my face is tired of holding up a fake smile
everyone is tricked into believing me
when i say i am okay.
i have mostly everyone fooled,
i even get responses like,
"i know you are okay"
"you know how to take care of yourself"

i force a smile extra hard to those responses
making sure my eyes do not meet theirs
as i know my eyes always tell the truth
i know if they get one glimpse of my eyes
all my tricks will be discovered

- *e.s*

i stay quiet.
i will no longer waste my breath,
explaining my story, opening up to people
people who use my memories and past as a weapon
against me.

i stay quiet.
i will no longer give my entire attention and love to others
filling them with kindness, with compassion
just for them to leave me completely empty.

    -   *e.s*

to me you're like a drug
everytime i see you

i want more
you make me feel so good

yet you're so harmful for me
it's so addicting
but it seems like i'm trapped

    - *e.s*

HEART ON PAPER

the problem with being so young
but filled with so much darkness,
is that no one takes you seriously,
no one thinks someone so young
could experience darkness,
they speak to me as if i chose the darkness,
as if i don't lay silently hoping the darkness lifts from my chest,
but i'm so young,
what do i know about life.
right?

- *e.s*

HEART ON PAPER

never let others make you feel
like your feeling aren't valid
even if others have it "worse" than you
your feelings matter
no matter what
if it hurts you
it hurts you
end of discussion

   - *letter to the reader*

HEART ON PAPER

so foolish of me to allow you to
convince me that i deserved
the things you said to me

so foolish of me to allow you
into manipulating me into
keeping you a secret

if you were worth my love
you wouldn't of asked me
to lie for you,
to forgive you for all the nights you screamed at me
taking out all your pain on me

if you were worth my love
then why have i spent countless nights crying in my room
alone
skipping events just to go and clean up your mess

i picked you up from the ground
i let you step all over me to get you to the top

i know better now

    -   *e.s*

why do i still feel this way?
i did everything right,

i took care of my health
i started therapy
i cut out old habits and toxic relationships
i surround myself with positive people
what else do i need to do?

-   *e.s*

HEART ON PAPER

there is so much i want to say
i just don't know where to start

there is so many people that tell me they are
here for me
and while i know that they most likely mean it
i am too afraid to reach out and ask for help

- *e.s*

i've realized why i am not fully healing
i've just been distracting myself

i've been pushing everything under the rug
instead of taking the time to actually face it all

    -   *e.s*

i wish i was enough for you,
i wish i could believe you when you say
there is nothing more important than me

but you don't look at me the same way
you look at drugs

- *e.s*

the person i was before,

i miss you.

    - *the person i am after*

you will never be small,
not with a heart as big as yours.
you will never fade,
not with a smile as bright as yours.
you will never be weak,
not with the battles your eyes have seen.
    - *letters to the readers*

HEART ON PAPER

if you ask anyone about me
they would not tell you that i am a dark person

they would tell you
i light up a room
i am radiant
i am the sun

and in a sense i am,
i am both the sun and the moon

no matter what battles my brain is facing,
i continue to be light even when it is dark.

your mental state does not define you,
you are not identified by what you have gone through
the beauty and radiance you hold will outshine any demon
within you

flowers still grow at night

    -   e.s

HEART ON PAPER

give yourself love when everything is going right,
when you did everything you said you would do,
and are accomplishing everything you put your mind to.

but also give yourself love when all is falling apart,
when life is continually challenging you,
when life is laughing at you for continuously breaking,

give yourself love.
you still deserve love when it is dark.

you are meant to be here
even on the days you feel like an outsider
home is something you deserve
never forget that

the earth is meant to have you in it
you belong here

    - *letter to the reader.*

thank you for reading my heart

- emma serio

Emma Serio

About the Author:

I was born in Milan, Italy and moved to the United States when I was six years old. There were so many emotions and changes throughout my life and when I began to learn the english language, I turned to journaling as a way to express what I was going through. I never stopped writing once I picked up the pencil, when there was no one to turn to, I turned to my journal and wrote for hours. I discovered the art of poetry when I was thirteen in my classroom when we were assigned a poetry project. It changed my life. It took my writing to a new level. I loved being able to tell my stories and experiences in a way that made people feel what I was feeling. When I decided to write this book I did it because I know I am not the only one who has gone through similar experiences, and I believe that everyone should be able to have something they may be able to relate too. There is no better feeling then when you feel heard, when you feel seen, when something you experienced or a feeling is put into words perfectly for you. I hope that is achieved through my poems for my readers. I want everyone to feel heard, to feel important.

~ Emma Serio